A Thousand Paths to Patience

A Thousand Paths to
patience

Michael Powell

MQP

Contents

Introduction

In a world where instant reward and the shortcuts to delight increasingly obscure the bigger picture, patience can sometimes seem little more than a cheerless compromise, a way to salve our disappointments. In fact, it is the true path to finding the essence of who we are and achieving our dreams.

How many possibilities do you see around you? When we cultivate patience they are endless, not least because it embraces a horde of other enviable qualities: hope, tolerance, compassion, tranquillity, and self-possession.

Patience is in the tiny details, while it is also to believe in something bigger than ourselves. It teaches us to take responsibility for our actions and our feelings; to forgive the imperfections, weaknesses, and fragility of ourselves and others; and above all, no matter how big the obstacles, it urges us never to give up.

Here within these pages we shall encounter patience in all its different aspects. As you read this book, one thing will become apparent—patience can enrich our lives every day, and should not be reserved merely for moments of crisis. It helps us to grow, to see below the surface, to harmonize with all those around us, and even to achieve the impossible.

What is Patience?

We've all been given one life. It's ours to do with as we please— for as long as it lasts.

Relax and get to know yourself. Try to understand life and your part in it. But take it slowly.

Breathe out the old day and breathe in the new. We're on our way to a long life. A life takes as long as it takes. If you've got nothing to do, what is life for?

The purpose of life
is to have a life
of purpose.

Patience is often born of necessity, but should be developed without obligation.

Patience should include a modicum of risk—trust always does.

Patience is sitting back
instead of hitting back.

Don't throw away a broken
relationship; instead spend
time trying to mend it.

Wanting things done yesterday often means that they don't get started until tomorrow. It's hard to begin a task with enthusiasm when you have already missed your own self-imposed deadline.

Forgive yourself your imperfections, weaknesses, and fragility, and you have taken the first step toward changing them.

A handful of patience is worth more than a bushel of brains.

Danish proverb

**There is no such thing
as a hopeless case.**

You must like people and be
patient with them if you want
to be surrounded by friends.

The remedy is not
always the cure.

In our lives five percent of our difficulties are brought about by circumstances out of our control, and ninety-five percent are caused by our own impatience.

A patient heart is better than all the guts, brains, and charisma in the world.

Patience is found in attentive and disciplined action, not in the act of waiting to begin.

Patience is the ability to bite your tongue when someone tells you to be more patient.

Genius is only a greater aptitude for patience.

Georges-Louis Leclerc de Buffon

The supply of patience will never outstrip the demand.

Always be a little more patient than you think you can: that's patience.

You don't know how patient you can be until you try.

Patience is never wasted; it conserves, nourishes, and protects as it is expended.

The roots of all goodness
lie in the soil of patience.

Nothing is more deserving
than a patient heart.

**If you don't allow things
to happen, they will seek
out and happen to those
who do.**

Patience enables us to panel-beat life's dents and smooth over its scratches.

Life is a gift —unwrap it carefully.

Patience is the
support of weakness;
impatience the ruin
of strength.

Charles Caleb Colton

**Cultivate patience
by enlarging your
imagination.**

Always try to keep the larger picture in mind.

Many irritations don't really have a significant impact on us, so long as we keep them in perspective.

**Patience is the oil that takes
the friction out of life.**

If you have not linked
yourself to true
patience, you will
never understand the
art of peace.

Develop the urge
to do things more
patiently than
anybody else.

**Patience is the ballast of the soul
that will keep it from rolling and
tumbling in the greatest storms.**

Bishop John Henry Hopkins

Patience is not only something you feel; it's something you do.

There are five steps in seeking patience: silence, listening, accepting, practicing, and then teaching others.

Always accept advice
with pleasure and grace,
even if you have no
intention of taking it.

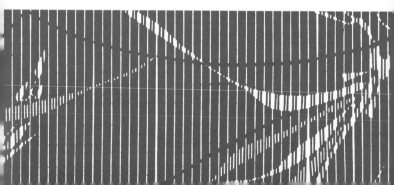

**Patience is not a skill.
It is an attitude.**

When we watch the animal
kingdom closely, we see the
special gift of patience in
many creatures.

The inner life—the life directed toward perfection—is a journey, and a certain preparation is necessary before you begin. If you are ill prepared, or act hastily, there is always the risk of having to return to the beginning before you have reached your destination.

Only patience can unravel the knots in the mind of our limited reason.

Amid the impetuous scamper and scurry of life, without patience the quality moments slip one by one into the shadows.

No school is more necessary to children than patience, because either the will must be broken in childhood or the heart in old age.

Johann Paul Richter

Watch your life change in perspective to the wonders you allow yourself the awareness to enjoy.

When you follow with patience doors will open where you would not have thought there would be doors.

Patience is more than just being patient. It is a connection deep within the spiritual soul that makes forbearing and unruffled perseverance the common threads that run through our lives.

Patience nourishes and facilitates all that your innermost spirit desires, for within patience you will discover the Creator's love.

How many possibilities do you see when you look around your world?

Make forgiveness your constant, unswerving companion.

Everything comes to him who hustles while he waits.
Thomas Edison

Patience is the shock absorber of life.

Patience comes into being when the brain discovers its fallibility and forgives itself.

If you can't be patient, you won't be anything much.

You have the power to spread tolerance today.

Nothing attracts patience like patience.

Patience allows you to attract the right people who will help you accomplish all your goals.

The only area that you are in complete control of is your mind.

Perhaps there is only one cardinal sin: impatience. Because of impatience we were driven out of Paradise, because of impatience we cannot return.

W. H. Auden

Patience is trust.

It is good to ask "why?" but it is even better to ask "why not?" because that is when we allow the magic to happen.

Patience is the intelligent channeling of human emotion.

**Don't get trapped
into doing too much.**

Do not create expectations in others
that you cannot fulfill; keep silent about
your plans until they reach fruition and
work unobtrusively until you have
arrived at your goal.

Making simple assumptions is a form of impatience that can damage relationships as well as your ability to make effective decisions.

Each person has far more patience than they have ever used.

Being patient and being spontaneous aren't mutually exclusive. Impatience makes us rigid, while patience helps us to leap out of our ruts, spurs us to change direction, and to find new ways to make our lives meaningful. Patience even gives us the courage to tear up our plans and start again.

It is in the everyday and the commonplace that we learn patience, acceptance, and contentment.

Richard J. Foster

Play the game to the best of your ability, regardless of your place in the lineup.

Everyone wants to win, but few are willing to invest the time and effort.

The most accomplished people in any field are those who are still the most eager to learn and improve.

There is enough to go wrong without sabotaging yourself.

You can't have a high-powered team with low-patience people.

Don't mistake movement for achievement.

Invest in time rather than spend it, and realize that it's never too late to begin anything.

I long to accomplish great and noble tasks, but it is my chief duty to accomplish humble tasks as though they were great and noble. The world is moved along, not only by the mighty shoves of its heroes, but also by the aggregate of the tiny pushes of each honest worker.

Helen Keller

Most people are about as impatient as they make up their mind to be.

Replace all your worry with patience, because although your patience may not solve all your problems, worry won't solve any of them.

Peak performance begins with patience.

Some people achieve little because they want to achieve everything, while others surpass their potential by acknowledging their limits.

There is no way to patience. Patience is the way.

Patience isn't granted, it is earned.

Patience may cost a lot, but it is the highest currency with which to purchase those things that truly matter.

If you had the choice between self-control and self-respect, choose the first because the second grows out of it.

What is patience but a private, personal, individual understanding of time as something organic and natural, and relative rather than something invented and manufactured and absolute?

Craig Russell

Don't lower your standards or expectations. The best things in life are worth the wait.

**Patience is always rewarded;
impatience is its own punishment.**

Patience isn't just going slowly or
standing still; it's also about
standing back.

**Nothing is perfect,
so don't expect it to be.**

Some name it destiny.
Some name it fate.
Others name it good luck.
Call it PATIENCE.

**Whatever life hands you,
good or bad, is still a gift.**

Patience is the sense of a solid
foundation and a buoyant future.

Patient people find solutions while the impatient ones are still searching for the problem.

Ask not what tomorrow may bring, but count as blessing every day that fate allows you.

Horace

Try not to postpone your happiness, for that is to postpone your life.

The less we do, the less we're able to do. If you want nothing, then do nothing.

Even in the most disagreeable situations you always have alternatives, if you have the courage to search for them.

Try combining your skills in different ways to come up with unusual results: same skills, different combinations and applications.

Patience is
in the details.

The question is not what we expect from life but rather, what life expects from us.

When you feel despair and discouragement, it is because you are frustrated by what you aren't getting; turn the problem on its head and figure out what you aren't giving.

Patience is part of the art of leadership, of getting along with people and making things happen.

**Enjoy what you can,
endure what you must.**

Johann Wolfgang von Goethe

Search within for the dignity of
mountains, the strength of winds, and
the perseverance of tides; seek the
unhewn, unfettered places of the heart
and you will find balance.

The impatient are
always in the wrong.

**Patience is like a garden
carried in the heart.**

You cannot make a living if you don't know how to smile.

Seeking the source of the river leads you away from the sea. Stay where you are and enjoy the water.

It is easier to pull down than to build up.

To endure is the first thing a child ought to learn, and that which he will have most need to know.

Jean-Jacques Rousseau

None of us can live forever, but we can make our lives appear longer by appreciating every minute.

The principal source of disappointment and sadness is exchanging what we want most for what we want right now.

Patience is the best means of persuasion.

Patience shows others what we are; so does impatience.

Patience is love in the solid form.

The impatient may not always be
wrong on issues, but they are almost
always wrong in their attitudes.

R. J. Rushdoony

**The next best thing to solving a
problem is to see the funny side.**

**Concentration and enquiry
are essential elements in
the art of patience.**

Pay attention to the coolness of the wind or the warmth of the sun on your cheeks, and smile.

There is nothing that we cannot use in order to practice patience. The only requirement is ourselves and a lucid and compassionate mind.

Confidently obey the eternal rhythm of life.

Things are never as bad as they appear; but they aren't any better either, so it's up to you how you take them.

You will never have a greater or lesser dominion than that over yourself.

Leonardo da Vinci

Like a boomerang, the consequences of impatience always come back to their origin.

A willingness to accept can often be the first step to effecting change.

The ultimate authority must always rest with your own composure and critical analysis.

Slow
Down
and See
Yourself

Learning to remove
all the haste in life
allows you to find
the essence of
who you are.

On your way to wherever you
are going, find beautiful things
to notice.

It is a continual barrage of hurly
-burly and urgency on which
we all spend ourselves that
keeps us from experiencing
who we truly are.

You must first have a lot
of patience to learn to
have patience.

Stanislaw J. Lec

Becoming who you are begins the process of finding your stillness among many.

There are two types of people: successful and impatient.

Patience makes a friend of time.

Accept that there is no need to rush yourself or others in facing the challenges of emotional growth.

Don't set your goals by what you think other people see as important. You are the only person who knows what is right for you.

The best and most beautiful things in the world cannot be snatched on the spur of the moment but are invited slowly into the heart.

Can you feel the wonder presented to you by a captured moment of stillness?

You are surrounded by miracles, if you take the time to look and feel their presence.

Find yourself by being nobody but yourself.

You pass this way only once, so why not take in the scenery?

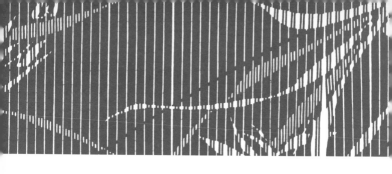

Have patience with all things, but
chiefly have patience with yourself.
Saint Frances de Sales

**If you want to see more
patience in the world,
exercise it.**

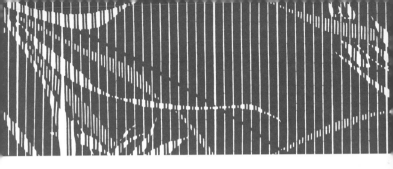

Follow your gut instinct but never rush into a decision.

Clear your mind of all the noise and upheaval of the modern world and make time stand still.

How much of human experience is misplaced through impatience, impulsiveness, and impetuosity?

When trouble arises that takes some time to resolve, resolve to take the trouble and the time.

The slower the pace, the longer the chase.

Direct all the energy you waste fretting about the slow pace of change into making those changes stick.

When other people won't change as quickly as you would like, it could be a sign that your need to change is greater than theirs.

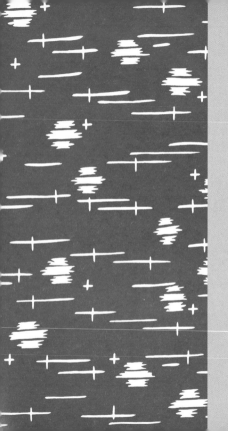

Patience is something you admire in the driver behind you and scorn in the one ahead.
  Mac McCleary

**Patience means changing
yourself before attempting
to change the world.**

Those who forever press ahead rarely
appreciate how far they have come.

**The only thing that patience allows
you to submit to is your true calling.**

**Slow down and pay
attention to your thoughts.**

Patience is the most efficient form of time management.

Be patiently alert to the creativity of each moment and be aware of what takes place in or outside yourself.

Adopt the pace of nature: her secret is patience.
Ralph Waldo Emerson

True patience is beyond time.

Impatient people feel as if
everything they do is too late.

**Spend more time
organizing your thoughts.**

If you want to live a life that
matters, develop your patience;
it will also teach you what it is
that matters.

Next time you tell yourself you should be able to do something faster, try slowing down and you'll be amazed by the results.

If you want others to be happy, start by being patient with them.

It is no small wonder that friction causes more heat than it does light. Patient judgement supplies light; hasty action only supplies heat.

A contented life must be to a great degree a patient life, for it is only in an environment of loving patience that true content can thrive.

Patience is the ability to idle your motor when you feel like stripping your gears.

Barbara Johnson

Those who lack the patience to answer questions are only marginally less foolish than those who are too impatient to ask them.

If you smile at the hard times, you will find it easier to laugh during the good times.

The biggest room in the world is the room for improvement.

Be patient with yourself; otherwise
how can you expect people to be
patient with you?

**Lack of patience leads to
frustration and self-loathing.**

Patience is the ability
to say no to oneself.

You have to find the peace and
patience within yourself to be a
model and an example to others
and not judge.

Judith Light

Patience strives for others; impatience strives for itself.

Always follow your instincts, but do it with patience and discipline.

If you don't show patience, how can you presume to deserve the patience of others?

Patience is like a twelve-speed bicycle—most of us have gears we never use.

You cannot force others to be patient; the best you can expect is to set an example.

Patience doesn't change things.
It changes people and they
change things.

Patience does not look at
the faults of others; it looks
toward self-improvement.

**Instead of pointing a finger,
we should hold out our hands.**

Trying to understand is like straining
through muddy water. Be still and
allow the mud to settle.

Lao Tzu

An impatient person
does not see the
same world that a
patient person sees.

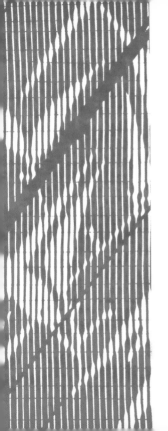

If you want to be liked, be patient with yourself.

Peace is not a goal or target; it occurs naturally when activity stops.

Impatience is an evasion of reality; patience is an acceptance of it. Only through acceptance can we begin to change reality.

Impatience, like a torrent, never looks back, and therefore can never learn from its mistakes.

Slow down so that you may give and receive encouragement.

By trying to force ourselves to grow we hinder our growth.

Patience, like charity, begins at home.

Act quickly, think slowly.

Greek proverb

Time shrinks to fit
our impatience.

**Some people go through a
forest and see no firewood.**

When you judge others, you don't
define them, you define yourself.

To a quick question
give a slow answer.

Everybody wants to be somebody, but few people have the patience to be themselves.

Without patience a person is unable to discern the consequences of their own actions.

Haste always seems to pursue those things which seem to be profitable for ourselves; pausing and saying "no" to this busyness enables us to understand what is best for the general good.

A selfless conscience, awakened by patient self-examination, leads to a peaceful and harmonious life.

Nature is a teacher which does not begin to teach until its pupil stops to listen.

Take your time. To be in a hurry is to kill your talent. If you wish to reach the sun it isn't enough to jump impulsively into the air.

Peter Ustinov

Every aspect of the life of an individual and of the life of the world has its ideal pace.

Impatience sees and yet does not look; hears and yet does not listen; touches and yet does not feel.

There's nothing wrong
with standing still;
a rock that stands
unmoved amid the
constantly moving
waves of the sea of
life becomes a rock
for others to lean on,
to depend upon.

Do not squander
your happiness
rushing around
searching in vain
for all the things
that cannot bring
you peace.

**The only thing we
can really change
is ourselves.**

Don't look for a change in circumstances; look for a change in character.

The thing that most frustrates our patience is not anger but ego.

Slow down and allow yourself to see the best in others.

Accept the pace at which the future arrives, regardless of whether it crawls or races toward the present.

They say that time changes things,
but you actually have to change
them yourself.

Andy Warhol

**No one can teach you
patience but yourself.**

Haste makes waste.

If you want patience, start thinking of yourself as a patient person and your actions will quickly bear out your thoughts.

A measured step is worth a hundred made in haste.

Impatience is the conviction that your time is more important than anyone else's.

The secret of patience is to overcome the biggest obstacle in your life before tackling the others; that obstacle is you.

Slow down; the past will catch up with you no matter how fast you run away from it.

Whenever you point the finger of blame at someone, there are three fingers pointing back at you.

Don't base every decision on what you think you see.

There is a way that nature speaks, that land speaks. Most of the time we are simply not patient enough, quiet enough, to pay attention to the story.

Linda Hogan

You're the only one in the world who can be the best that YOU can be.

With any task you need patience to spot the shortcuts.

The flame that burns the brightest burns out the soonest.

Sometimes a quick fix is fine so long as you recognize that it is a temporary solution.

Taking more time out
helps us to take more in.

Be aware of what you do well and use this awareness to bring you success; play to your strengths, and not your weaknesses.

If you won't let others be what they want to be, it is a sign that you need to let yourself be what you have always wanted to be.

Better to complete a small task well, than to do much imperfectly.

Plato

Make space in your life
to celebrate more often.

**With awareness and persistence
we can all gain greater mastery
over our emotional states.**

Those who are most out of control feel the greatest urge to control others.

Your self-image is your own choice.

Sharpen your patience by finding more opportunities to laugh, especially at yourself.

Patience and anger are not merely add-ons to your sense of self; they actually shape your personality.

In the name of God, stop a moment, cease your work, look around you.

Leo Tolstoy

Slow to anger, quick to understand.

Patience is within every heart, but only through learning to listen to your heart can the possibility of this patience be realized.

You can only perceive beauty with an unruffled mind.

Haste and impatience are always the best way to defeat our purposes.

When a butterfly
emerges from its
cocoon, its wings
must dry in the sun
for several hours
before it can fly.

Do not be in a hurry to do what you cannot undo.

Learn to be calm and you will always be patient.

It is impossible to walk with dignity when you are always in a hurry.

If a man is destined
to drown, he will
drown even in a
spoonful of water.

Yiddish proverb

When in doubt, slow down.

True victory
is self-victory.

**Stop and embrace
the essence of
who you are.**

Patience in your heart will take you to new places.

The fruit that
ripens soonest
rots soonest.

Do not allow time to pass unnoticed.

Being patient means looking beyond the imperfections of our lives.

Impatience to leave the starting blocks leads to false starts. The bird that flutters least is longest on the wing.

William Cowper

Remain
Calm

Stamping your foot is very different from making your mark.

The surest sign of weakness is retaliation.

Be slow to anger and quick to forgive.

The only way to heal anger is to generate peace; the only way to generate peace is to show patience and love.

Patience serves as a protection against wrongs as clothes do against cold. For if you put on more clothes as the cold increases, it will have no power to hurt you. So in like manner you must grow in patience when you meet with great wrongs, and they will then be powerless to vex your mind.

Leonardo da Vinci

Anger disguises our vulnerability; when someone has wronged you, if you react with anger, that is all they can see— they cannot see your hurt.

Patience is the greatest symptom of inner peace.

You cannot always avoid battles, but choose them carefully.

Patience doesn't only concern itself with conquering hate within; it uses its strength to fight hate without.

Meet both the expected and unexpected outcome without anxiety, tension, or annoyance.

Show me a person with little patience and I'll show you a person with even less respect.

What's the use of being angry at events? Events are just the things that have happened; focus on all the wonderful things that haven't happened yet, and make them come about.

For every minute you are angry you lose sixty seconds of happiness.
Ralph Waldo Emerson

Lose your patience, and lose a whole lot more besides.

He who makes you lose your patience makes you lose yourself.

Nothing sets a better example than composure.

People who approach life without losing their cool generate the most warmth.

A leader without patience soon finds himself with nobody to lead.

Impatience slams the door on the human spirit.

Those who fly into a rage often suffer a bad landing.

You don't have to attend every argument you're invited to.

If you are patient in one moment of anger, you will escape a hundred days of sorrow.

Chinese proverb

Anger makes you smaller, while patience makes you grow beyond that which others believe is possible.

If people don't understand you the first time, raise your game, not your voice.

The greatest pleasure in life is keeping your cool when others least expect it.

Show patience toward impatient people—they need it the most.

**Although the world is full of anger,
it is full also of the overcoming of it.**

Anger is the real sacrifice of self.

Your reputation is delicate as a glass: once broken by anger it can be fixed but there will always be cracks.

When you are backed into a corner, don't climb the walls.

No one can make you feel angry without your consent.

Beware the fury of a patient man.
John Dryden

The only way to cherish consciousness is to stay calm.

It is in moments of serenity that you truly understand the strength of your thoughts.

Those who wish to conquer the world are the angriest at it.

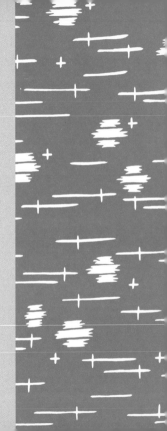

You are here for no other purpose than to manifest your innate enlightenment, so anger can never work toward that intention.

Rule your emotions or they will rule you.

Pain is inevitable; anger is optional.

Nothing can destroy your mental happiness and peace of mind except your own anger.

Patience is a tool of the peacemaker.

Our patience will achieve more than our force.

Edmund Burke

Use your irritating experiences to create pearls of forgiveness.

Learning to accept minor irritations prepares us to endure major ones.

Don't permit your life to be lessened by any moment of anger.

In truth, how many moments of true even-temperedness have you had?

Never pay back anger for anger to anyone.

Self-control is one of life's greatest pleasures; we are at our happiest when we feel in control of ourselves.

Whatever you are, be a mild-tempered one.

The ease with which we can develop anger should tell you all you need to know about its value.

One moment of patience may ward off great disaster. One moment of impatience may ruin a whole life.

Chinese proverb

Patience is the ability to listen
to almost anything without losing
your temper or your self-belief.

**We have a million reasons
for losing our temper, but
not a single excuse.**

Patience avoids the people and
situations you don't want easily and
effortlessly without any confrontations.

Patience allows you to let go of anger and start living the life you want.

Consider anger as another limiting thought pattern.

To display anger risks making you a greater doormat than showing patience.

People's reactions act as a mirror, reflecting our own tranquillity.

Patience improves communication and therefore greatly reduces the risk of the anger that results from breakdowns of communication.

If at first you don't succeed, don't, whatever you do, get angry about it.

If a small thing has the power to make you angry, does that not indicate something about your size?

Sydney J. Harris

It is easy to be an angel when nobody ruffles your feathers.

The essence of patience is saying no to frustration, anger, judgment, or blame.

Consider how much more you often suffer from your impatience than from the objects of your impatience.

People often make up with impatience what they lack in judgment.

Impatience begins with irritation and ends with regret.

When people offer you abuse, politely refuse to accept it and reply, "Now it belongs to you."

Anger is pride, therefore the humbler you are in your behavior, the happier and more patient you will feel.

There will be a time when loud-mouthed, incompetent people seem to be getting the best of you. When that happens, you only have to be patient and wait for them to self-destruct. It never fails.

Richard Rybolt

You can never achieve serenity and inner patience without first acknowledging all of the good things in your life.

Impatience is highly addictive and bad for your health, so quit now. Better still, don't start.

We are disturbed not by things but by the attitude we take toward them.

Overreaction leaves no room for effective action.

If no anger,
then no enemy.

Peace begins with you.

Don't get angry with yourself; there are plenty of people out there who will bring their anger to you, without you joining in.

No man can think clearly when his fists are clenched.

George Jean Nathan

Every opportunity to develop anger presents the same opportunity to develop patience.

Biting your lip is infinitely preferable to biting somebody's head off.

When we feel resentment it is not relevant to the present moment, it is reacting to a past pain.

Rein in your anger or hand the reins of your freedom to someone else.

Feeling crushed and bitter because of a
failure is worse than the failure itself.

**Invest all your energy in
whatever brings you peace.**

**You will have peace
only if you are a part
of something peaceful.**

The test of good manners is
to be patient with bad ones.
Solomon Ibn Gabirol

**Consider it your duty
to increase the peace.**

**The words of the patient are
spoken softly and peacefully.**

**One minute of patience,
ten years of peace.**

Greek proverb

Use the appropriate words to express
your feelings and don't exaggerate.
Sloppy language leads to heightened
feelings such as irritation and anger.
It is possible to talk yourself into an
agitated frame of mind simply by
resorting to hyperbole.

The world is driven by action, not silence; nevertheless all your social engagements should be actuated by serenity.

Remember, what you put out comes back, whether it is anger or mild-temperedness.

What angers you masters you.

The reputation of a thousand
years may be determined by
the conduct of one hour.

Japanese proverb

**Which do you think wastes
the most time and energy:
losing your temper or
counting to twenty?**

If you are not taking away from the chaos and incoherence that is around you, then you are adding to it.

Having an even temper means never having to get even.

Anger may solve a problem in the short-term, but it sows the seeds for another.

Gentleness is the only way.

Those who are easily offended make the best offenders.

If you want to see virtue,
you have to have a calm mind.

Keep cool; anger is not an argument.
Daniel Webster

Adversity should make a
person patient, not angry.

Avoid antagonism
and it will avoid you.

**The best response
to anger is silence.**

It takes two flints to make a fire.

Louisa May Alcott

**When we stop flapping, we
exchange the impossibility of
flight for the rapture of gliding.**

Show even temper to those who are near, and those who are far will quickly learn of your serenity.

Never carry out with your fists what you can achieve with your words; never seek with your words what you can attain with your silence.

You will not be punished for your anger; you will be punished by your anger.

Buddha

By all means write letters when you are angry, but you don't have to post them.

Anger opens the window on all of your faults.

Two cannot argue if one does not choose.

There is no such thing as an insignificant anger.

Fear is usually the greatest cause of impatient behavior and intolerance.

Patience means wrapping a soft layer of clemency around your words.

What can be so bad about anyone that they deserve your terrible temper?

If you are not calm, your fate depends on those who are calmer.

To rule one's anger is well; to prevent it is still better.

Tyron Edwards

It's not what was said that matters, but how you took it.

Try a little patience today; you can always get angry tomorrow.

The inevitable will happen, whether you get upset about it or not.

Those who allow themselves to be driven by anger can never get out of the passenger seat.

Wherever your anger leads you, you'll need all the patience you can muster to find your way back.

We should remember that every opportunity to develop anger is also an opportunity to develop patience.

Geshe Kelsang Gyatso

Everything that annoys us about others can help us to understand ourselves.

Patience can move mountains, but anger will create them.

Why be angry? The moment has already passed.

Resentment is like taking poison and waiting for the other person to die.

If you can't decide between hate and love, choose the one that feels better afterward.

Make it your absolute rule that anger is unacceptable.

Keep your anger to yourself, but share your serenity with others. The practice of patience does not consist in weakly giving in to oppression but in that which squarely opposes the chief oppressor, our own anger.

The Dalai Lama

Problems
Lead to
Success

If you have the patience to stay alert, positive and open, then when a unique opportunity finally presents itself to you, not only will you recognize its potential, but you will also have the necessary reserves of energy to take action.

Patience is the key to the gate of happiness.

Patience is not the absence of conflict but allows the formation of creative alternatives for responding to it.

Patience gives you the ability to transform problems into opportunities.

Our real blessings often appear to us in the shape of pains, losses, and disappointments; but let us have patience and we soon shall see them in their proper figures.

Joseph Addison

Patience is the tireless alchemy which transforms talent into genius.

Setbacks, delays, and reversals are inevitable components of forward motion.

Patient exercise of the will is the only way to develop your potential.

Patience is not only the greatest of virtues, but the parent of all others.

If you bite off more than you can chew, don't make the mistake of thinking that all you lack is a bigger mouth.

Patience is the bridge between goals and accomplishment.

Follow through when everyone else is content to just follow.

Patience is not merely to wait and see what will happen; it is the unruffled appreciation that comes after the event, like a golfer watching his ball sail through the air after striking a flawless drive.

Patience is the highest expression of potency.

When patience frames your mental landscape, the beauty of the world will be revealed to you.

There's a tendency for those without restraint to interpret every setback as a setup.

Knowing trees, I understand the meaning of patience. Knowing grass, I can appreciate persistence.

Hal Borland

Impatience can sometimes be the spur to action, but most often it paralyzes creativity and compounds disquietude.

Let your patience release all your frustrated possibilities.

Patience walks hand in hand with personal responsibility.

Good enough isn't good enough; try again.

Many a man thinks he is patient when, in reality, he is indifferent.

B. C. Forbes

Don't give up on your dreams. Where there is passion and patience, you can't go wrong.

A failure is a man who is too impatient to learn from his mistakes.

When you come to a roadblock, getting angry at the detour does nothing to speed up your journey. After every setback in your life, keep calm and put your energy into finding an alternative course of action.

Beware lest you lose a fresh opportunity by mourning the loss of the last one.

Chance will enable you to find a solution every once in a while, but patient and consistent achievement removes luck from the equation.

With ordinary talents and
extraordinary patience,
all things are within reach.

If you don't make a few mistakes along
the way, you won't make anything.

All human errors are impatience, a premature breaking off of methodical procedure, an apparent fencing-in of what is apparently at issue.

Franz Kafka

Plants need rain to grow and so do people.

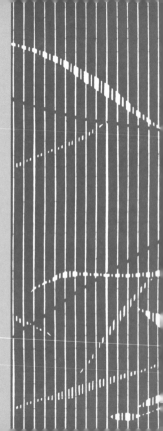

It is in your moments of patience that your destiny is shaped.

Patience or impatience: which one do you want to determine your future?

Go patiently in the direction of your dreams.

Patience unlocks the infinite possibilities that lie undiscovered and unrecognized about us.

Those who give up on patience give up on seeking the truth.

Better to do nothing patiently than to do something impatiently.

A moderate idea that is pursued with poise will go further than a grand idea that is pushed at the world with terse apprehension.

We could never learn to be brave and patient, if there were only joy in the world.

Helen Keller

A person can succeed at almost anything with which he has unlimited patience.

One person has patience for thirty minutes, another for thirty days, but it is the person who has it for fifty years who makes a success of his life.

A musician must make music, an artist must paint, a poet must write; but if they are to be any good, they must all have patience.

Patience takes constant practice; fortunately life offers plenty of opportunities to do just that.

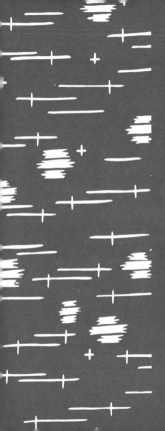

Our patience should increase in direct proportion to the obstacles placed before us.

Misfortune is something we all have to endure from time to time.

Patience is an affirmation of the dignity of humanity, an avowal to overcome whatever obstacles confront us.

If we begin with certainties, we shall end in doubts. But if we begin with doubts, and are patient in them, we shall end in certainties.

Francis Bacon

A problem is a chance for you to test your patience.

Sometimes patience is the only choice you can make, until other choices become available.

When you set out on a journey and fog covers the road, you don't decide that the road has vanished. Be patient and the fog will disperse.

Patience affords you the space to generate your own circumstances.

Your past does not equal your future.

Patience is the most effective form of positive thinking.

Patience leads to better outcomes because it allows us to consider more options and ask more questions.

If we were to live patiently, our lives would heal themselves.

Patience decides the size of our dreams.

Anyone who proposes to do good must not expect people to roll stones out of his way, but must accept his lot calmly if they even roll a few more upon it.

Albert Schweitzer

Impatience trips over obstacles in its path; patience removes them so that others do not make the same mistake.

Sometimes it can feel as though blind chance guides us to different destinations in life, but patience sets our sail.

Learn to view failures as temporary inconveniences.

Make decisions and act untiringly in the face of setbacks.

Impatient thinking dwells on limitations and impossibilities; patience looks beyond them.

Patience is both a sign and a generator of positive self-esteem.

Without patience lives are lost and dreams are destroyed.

Difficulties increase the nearer we get to the goal.

Goethe

A rock may change the river's course, but it does not change the river.

Your mind may be the biggest obstacle you will ever face. If you can control that, just think what you can achieve.

Don't avoid your problems;
get through them.

**Remember, an amateur
built the Ark; professionals
built the *Titanic*.**

**To a great extent, our
patience is only limited
by our own expectations.**

Destiny is not a matter of chance;
it is a matter of patience.

Be content to view the success of others for what it is and not as a negative comment on your own life.

There are two ways to live your life: with patience or impatience, and each creates wildly different results.

All things good to
know are difficult
to learn.

Without rain a desert will form.

**To him that waits all things reveal
themselves, provided that he
has the courage not to deny,
in the darkness, what he has
seen in the light.**

Coventry Kersey Dighton Patmore

Sometimes you have to walk through puddles, instead of waiting for the ground to dry.

**If you plant thorns,
don't expect to gather roses.**

Impatience feels like rowing upstream: if you are not going forward you feel as if you are dropping back.

The experiences that teach us the most are the ones we haven't bargained for.

Everything is not always about you.

Patience helps us to cope with the punctures on the wheel of life.

Don't let your dreams be destroyed by shallow illusions.

Challenges are sent to knock us down so we can learn how to get back up.

Life without patience is a life without direction. If your life has no patience, what is your focus?

Failure doesn't mean that you're a failure...it just means that you haven't succeeded yet.

Robert Schuler

Your ability to make brave decisions
while under criticism is called patience.

**When things don't go as planned,
ask questions rather than
demand answers.**

You can't face adversity by
turning your back on it.

Instead of saying, "Why did this happen to me?" ask, "Why was I selected for this opportunity?"

It's easier to fly if you take things lightly.

Impatience is a thief that steals our well-being.

In the confrontation between the stream and the rock, the stream always wins, not through strength but by perseverance.

H. Jackson Brown

How on earth would we raise our game if we didn't have obstacles in our path?

We are put on earth to develop patience.

The patient life helps
a soul grow up.

The secrets of earth and heaven
are revealed to those who wait.

When we abandon
patience, we abandon
talent, growth, and
self-discipline.

Try to imagine time in terms of quality rather than quantity.

The first thing you should do before attempting to grow anything is cultivate patience.

Impatience and reason cancel each other out.

You won't find yourself unless you are first prepared to make yourself.

Do you have patience to wait till your mud settles and the water is clear? Can you remain unmoving till the right action arises by itself?

Lao Tzu

Many of the most tragic examples of human error can be traced back to a single moment of impatience.

Don't worry! Be patient.

The biggest lesson we can demonstrate to our children is patience.

Impatience extinguishes the lamp of the mind.

Great patience takes great courage.

People never improve unless they increase their tolerance to the unfamiliar, their resistance to defeat, and their persistence in the face of seemingly unworkable options.

Patience makes it through whatever comes along.

Nothing is as strong as patience, and nothing is as patient as true strength.

**If you can't change your
fate, change your attitude.**

Amy Tan

One of the greatest pains
to human nature is the
pain of impatience.

Sometimes patience means having the courage to cut your losses and move on.

The storm is only temporary. What creates a lasting impression is the marvel you experience when the sun bursts through the clouds and begins to shine once more.

Patience cannot heal sorrows
but it makes them lighter to bear.

**Impatience may give you
a short burst of energy to
get things done, but it
steals far more energy
than it provides.**

Time is a created thing. To say, "I don't have time," is like saying, "I don't want to."

Lao Tzu

Don't mistake the ladder of success for an escalator. You must do the climbing.

**Small opportunities for
self-control are often
the beginning of
great undertakings.**

Use your patience as
a beacon to light up
the darkest corners
of the world.

It is hard to accept
with humility that
which is offered;
it is even harder to
accept with serenity
that which is denied.

Tolerance and perseverance
are necessities, not luxuries.

It's Worth
the Wait

Anything worth having is worth the wait.

Impatience is living for the results rather than focusing wholeheartedly on the actions that can achieve them.

The most worthwhile things cannot always be completed during a single lifetime.

How we endure today determines the quality of tomorrow.

Always wait your turn, even when there isn't enough to go around.

Truth is power, but only when one has patience and requires of it no immediate effect.
　　Romano Guardini

The longer the wait,
the weightier the reward.

Let go of your need
for immediate results.

Like grapes on the vine,
joys postponed are sweeter
than those reaped in haste.

If everything happened at once, what would be left?

Those who seek an immediate payoff for their hard work are the same ones who run up debts before they receive it.

Patient people may feel as though they are being overlooked, but patience is always noticed and respected.

Teach us, O Lord, the disciplines of patience, for to wait is often harder than to work.

Peter Marshall

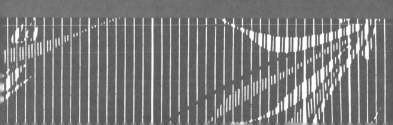

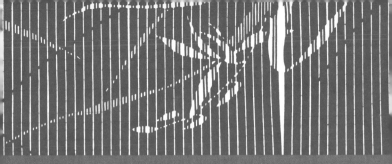

Patience often requires us to postpone the attainment of things, but never the attainment of happiness.

Demanding the impossible is not impatience; demanding it immediately—now that's impatience.

Be optimistic about the future, but above all be patient with the present.

Patience teaches us to wait until tomorrow for what we don't deserve today.

Expecting immediate rewards is as unrealistic and shameful as demanding a free meal every time you visit a restaurant.

The quality of a person's life is in direct proportion to their ability to delay gratification, regardless of the undertaking.

If you're a patient person you'll have no trouble in appreciating the success of others, even if it comes before your own.

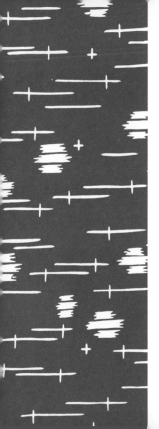

Never look at what you have left; always look at what you still have to offer.

If you would know strength and patience, welcome the company of trees.

Hal Borland

A taste for simplicity allows tolerance and patience to grow.

Where there is patience, there is always a handful of wishes kept busy.

**Patience is living
for a cause that
outlives your life.**

Patience frees us to
act according to the
circumstances,
rather than our
expectations.

Do something now that will help you in the future.

Remember time brings roses.

The best things in life don't happen at the touch of a button.

Don't pull up the
flowers to see
how the roots
are doing.

**Do not seek
answers for which
you are not ready,
because you will
not be able to live
them yet.**

There are no honors too distant to the man who prepares himself for them with patience.

Jean de la Bruyère

Patience is a commitment to the future.

Your life depends upon the care with which you plant the seeds of your future.

Don't follow the path, clear a new one. It will take longer but the rewards will be tenfold.

Patience is the only road to true freedom, and self-mastery is its ultimate reward.

Real,
constructive
mental
fortitude
lies in the
creative
withstanding
that shapes
your destiny.

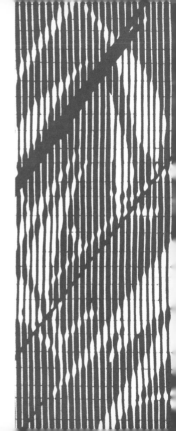

Allow your quiescent instincts to take over your restive instincts and provide the engine to become greater.

The task ahead of us should never be greater than the patience behind us.

Patient words create a world full of possibilities, while impatient ones shrink the opportunities available to us.

Trust and accept that things will work out in the end.

Spend as much time laying the foundations for your dreams as you do building them.

The key to everything is patience.
You get the chicken by hatching
the egg, not by smashing it.

Arnold H. Glasow

Your patience
creates
everything in
your life.

Exercising five minutes' more patience each day can change your life.

With patience you will learn that you are exactly where you need to be and that you got there because of past decisions and emotions.

The only way to get immediate results is to exercise more patience.

Don't get impatient because you can't have it all. We all have to choose what we can have.

Failure doesn't mean God has abandoned you; it means He has a better idea.

Patient people always see the future in the present.

Reflect more, risk more, and invest in ventures that are bigger and more enduring than your own existence.

When you are truly ready for a thing, it usually shows up.

Patience is necessary, and one cannot reap immediately where one has sown.

Søren Kierkegaard

Do not put off your enjoyment until you have more time, or money, or a better job, or some other improved circumstance. Start enjoying yourself right now.

Patience is planting a garden for your grandchildren to enjoy.

To receive everything, one must open one's heart and wait.

Creativity is tolerating the unfinished long enough for you to sprinkle magic on it.

Never look at how long you have left; always look at why you are waiting and whether it matches your requirements.

Patience is to
believe in
something
bigger than you.

Eating the corn stalks is not nearly as satisfying as eating the corn.

Don't throw the ball
before you have it.
Vernon Law

Sure there's always tomorrow, but what's wrong with now?

As far as possible,
be mindful of the long-term
consequences of your actions.

Plant trees so future generations can enjoy the shade.

Don't wait until night time to declare you've had a good day; it should be the first decision you make upon waking.

Every man must patiently bide his time. He must wait—not in listless idleness but in constant, steady, cheerful endeavors, always willing and fulfilling and accomplishing his task, that when the occasion comes he may be equal to the occasion.

Henry Wadsworth Longfellow

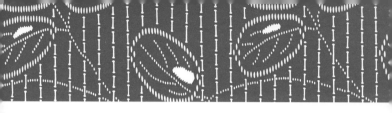

Patience enables us to be the person we thought we would become when we grew up.

Be willing to allow the divine to unfold as it should without getting in its way.

Every day could be the day you've been waiting for.

As you are traveling down your road, don't look down at your feet.

Infinite
patience
brings
immediate
results.
    Wayne Dyer

Remove the expectations from what you give and share.

What do you want to look back on?

If you chase
two rabbits,
both will escape.

**Don't expect a great day;
make one.**

**There is nothing like patience
to create a better future.**

Think of all the consequences
that are waiting for you.

Patience allows you to achieve peace despite the difficulties of life, rather than to postpone well-being until after you have conquered all your troubles, delaying happiness forever.

Patience is an opportunity, not an obligation.

A dream can be nurtured over years
and years and then flourish rapidly...
Be patient. It will happen for you.
Sooner or later, life will get weary of
beating on you and holding the door
shut on you, and then it will let you in
and throw you a real par.

Lester Louis Brown

If everyone waited their turn and took no more than their share, there would be no famine, poverty, or global warming.

Patience brings quiet joy.

We can only create
what we can anticipate.

**Give proof to others of your
patience by your actions.**

The best possession you can
have is self-possession.

**Those who only show patience
when they have no other choice,
limit their choices in all the other
areas of their life.**

Anyone who stops learning is old; anyone who stops showing patience is like an unruly and unteachable child.

Self-determination should always be tempered with self-control.

Allow your even-tempered moments to create the world of your dreams.

The man for whom time stretches out painfully is one waiting in vain, disappointed at not finding tomorrow already continuing yesterday.

Theodor Adorno

None of us are born with patience. A baby cries and demands its needs to be met immediately. An adult who expects the same has a lot of emotional growing up to do. Have you grown up yet?

Shift your focus from your desires to your responsibilities, and you will achieve both.

The loss of patience is by no means the most pernicious loss that a human being can experience, but it is the most unnecessary.

Anything that contradicts the instincts of compassion and restraint should be abandoned.

The closest thing to being free is the ability to accept whatever life throws at you with good humor.

Never cut short your waiting with compromise. Simply put, the waiting's not over until the waiting's done.

Duke Rohe

Be kind to your enemies—
you made them.

An impatient person deserves pity but rarely gets it.

To build patience is to build mastery.

Happiness is optional.

Patience is not something you wish for; it's something you make.

Don't wait for the wrong things.

Anything worth chasing is worth waiting for.

Nothing in this world is owed to you; you have to bring it in.

Patience! The windmill never strays in search of the wind.

Andy J. Sklivis

The journey is the reward.

Patience is not relaxing too early, not getting too comfortable.

Expect a lot, but take what is offered.

Don't fight the waves; wait for the good ones and ride them.

Patience is surrendering yourself to your highest spiritual purpose.

Not only is impatience unrewarding, it's also exhausting.

Patience enables us to act spontaneously rather than on our fears.

Stop delaying and denying what you are passionate about.

**Patience is giving up the
search for a better past.**

You can't expect things to
happen just because you
want them to.

**Patience isn't something we
get out of life;
it's something we put into it.**

Unless our lives are framed
by patience, contentment
is out of the picture.

Step by Step

Every "Eureka!" moment is preceded
by years of patient application.

Patience is the result of habit.
We become patient by
showing patience hour
by hour, day by day; the
way we spend each day
is the way we spend our lives.

Patience is not the same as apathy; the actions of patient people are effective because they are not discouraged when results come slowly and they sustain their belief that their actions will yield the desired outcome.

Patience concerns itself with making small daily achievements, which add up to big lifetime achievements.

The sea does not reward those who are too anxious, too greedy, or too impatient. To dig for treasures shows not only impatience and greed, but also lack of faith. Patience, patience, patience, is what the sea teaches. Patience and faith. One should lie empty, open, choiceless as a beach —waiting for a gift from the sea.

Anne Morrow Lindbergh

Achieve the impossible by patiently breaking it down into dollops of can-do.

Patience conquers all in the end.

The most beautiful things in the world reveal themselves slowly.

There is no value in reaching your goals if you burn yourself out to achieve them.

Patience is the ability to set realistic short-term targets and taking one day at a time in order to reach your bigger goals.

The art of living lies less in eliminating our troubles than in growing with them.

Bernard M. Baruch

Show resignation in the little things in order to achieve the bigger things.

Gradually changing and growing daily endures longer than being an overnight sensation.

The next time you want something to fall into your lap, try sitting down.

Find patience in the breath of life.

Ryunosuke Satoro

You have to take life one day at a time, because how else do you think your life is going to play out?

**An oak tree is the result
of an acorn's patient
effort to reach the sky.**

Constant and determined patience
breaks down all opposition and
brushes away all impediments.

Patience is also a form
of action.

Auguste Rodin

Motivation is what gets you out
of bed in the morning. Patience
is what keeps you awake.

Little by little achieves a lot.

Impatience sprints down the path of least resistance.

You can learn new things at any time in your life if you're willing to be patient.

Beware of endeavouring to become a great man in a hurry. One such attempt in ten thousand may succeed. These are fearful odds.

Benjamin Disraeli

You can never show patience too soon, because you never know how soon it will be too late.

Things only get better over time when those with patience and vision bring about positive change; otherwise things tend to stay the same or get worse.

With time and patience the mulberry leaf becomes a silk gown.

Patience must be consistent and continuous; otherwise it is merely occasional tolerance.

Nature takes away any inherent ability that is not used; practice patience all the time.

**An ounce of patience is worth
a pound of ambition.**

Keep on keeping on and
express gratitude daily.

**Patience maintains momentum,
while impatience destroys it.**

A falling drop at last will carve a stone.

Lucretius

Patience is like a flower;
give it time and it will grow.

There are no
shortcuts to doing
a good job.

**The future belongs to
those who have the
patience to create it.**

Have the patience to do your best today and whatever you achieve, remember that tomorrow is another day.

Absence of actions is as far removed from patience as a vacant mind.

Each small
of patience
changes the
world in some
unseen way.

... day anew by clothing ... patience.

... merely a distant goal that we seek, but a means by which we arrive at that goal.

If you patiently seek your real purpose in life you will be sought by that purpose.

We shall escape the uphill by never turning back.

Christina Rossetti

Patience and sincerity lead straight to the goal.

Patience enables us in every situation, in every facility, to answer the demands of the moment.

Promise sincerity, command trust, and spread goodness, day after day.

A patient person may take one step outwardly; inwardly they have taken a thousand.

Who is there that, shooting all day long, does not sometimes hit the mark?

Learn the art of patience. Apply discipline to your thoughts when they become anxious over the outcome of a goal. Impatience breeds anxiety, fear, discouragement, and failure. Patience creates confidence, decisiveness, and a rational outlook, which eventually leads to success.

Brian Adams

The patient weak ones will always conquer the impatient strong.

Instead of focusing on what needs to be done, turn your attention to what you can create with the moments you are given.

Doing your patient best in this moment is the best preparation for the next moment.

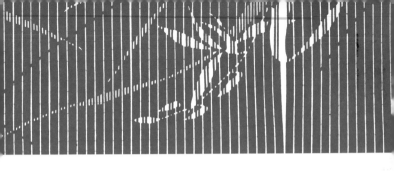

The crowded hours
come to you always
one moment at a time.

Inspire greatness in the next
generation by helping them to
face day-to-day challenges.

The hundredth blow cannot split
the stone without the ninety-nine
that come before.

**Patience is a canvas furnished
by discipline and garnished
by soft-heartedness.**

**How poor are they who
have not patience!
What wound did ever
heal but by degrees.**
    William Shakespeare

Carefully observe which way your heart directs you, and then follow that trail with untiring tenacity.

Passion launches great works; patience alone completes them.

Never think that God's delays are God's denials. Hold on; Hold fast; Hold out. Patience is genius.

Georges-Louis Leclerc Buffon

Patiently seek to acquire knowledge and do not allow yourself to be led by superficial beliefs and dogmas.

Nature rarely creates change in an instant.

Do you want what you don't have or what you can't have?

At the core of every true talent there is an awareness of the difficulties inherent in any achievement, and the confidence that by persistence and patience something worthwhile will be realized.

Eric Hoffer

Patience means always finding a way to keep yourself actively working toward your ambition.

Don't worry about the future. Focus on accomplishing what's right in front of you right now.

Remember that overnight success
usually takes at least fifteen years.

**Instead of wasting time learning the
tricks of a trade, learn the trade.**

Each day expect a little more
from yourself than yesterday.

Patient people enjoy the
journey rather than daydream
about the destination.

It takes a lifetime to become the person we want to be.

Only those who have the patience to do simple things perfectly ever acquire the skill to do difficult things easily.

It's a war of attrition. If you have patience and a modicum of faith in yourself your chances are not too bad.

Julie Bowen

Patience is the ability to count down before you blast off.

So long as you are walking in the right direction with patience, you will arrive.

No mountain is too big for you to move, so long as you remember to pick up one stone at a time.

Impatience is concerned with how quickly we move toward our goal. Patience is concerned with how we move toward our goal.

Life is a blank canvas: throw as much color on it as you like, but remember to stand back and let the paint dry from time to time, otherwise you'll just end up with a grubby mess.

**Success is always
closer than you think.**

Think big, but
start small.

**It takes time to understand
all of life's lessons.**

Good ideas are not adopted automatically. They must be driven into practice with courageous patience.

Hyman Rickover

Look around you, determine what needs to be done, start doing it.

Break down your obstacles and your goals.

Every drop of rain makes the river stronger.

You have to have your goal in mind before you can begin your first steps toward it.

Live from moment to moment and don't fall down the cracks in between.

Take the time to rehearse success.

Ripples travel just as far as waves.

It is by attempting to reach the top in a single leap that so much misery is produced in the world.

William Cobbett

It doesn't matter when others get ahead of you. There will always be someone else in front.

Deal with difficult challenges one step at a time.

Divide all your problems into smaller, more manageable chunks.

Make certain that the next moment you bring about is the greatest you can possibly create.

Accepting a defeat lessens the chances of having to accept the next one.

Don't see things as they are; see
them as you want them
to be, and then make them so.

**Day after day, attempt to
contribute to the beauty
and prosperity of the world.**

Don't be afraid of growing slowly;
be afraid only of standing still.

**Patience can't be acquired
overnight. It is just like building
up a muscle. Every day you need
to work on it.**

Eknath Easwaran

Time gives good advice.

Accept that you have progressed and will continue to do so.

Winners are not made at the finish line, but in the months of preparation leading up to the race.

Whatever you are involved with, apply yourself until you are in the position to make announcements, not excuses.

Complete involvement during the
process saves corrections after.

**The people on top of the
mountain did not fall there.**

Be prepared to repeat yourself:
it's the only way to get people to listen.

The things that are most important are hidden from us until we gain the fortitude to invite them into our lives.

In the struggle between the stone and the water, in time, the water wins.

Chinese proverb

It is primarily with their own selves that people are impatient.

No one hammers a nail with one blow.

Patiently continue to do what is right in all situations.

Like a muscle, patience must be exercised every day, otherwise it begins to atrophy.

Act with patience and in time you will become patient.

We are never more impatient with others than when we are impatient with ourselves.

Become addicted to constant and never-ending self-control.

There are two things a person should never be impatient at: what they can help, and what they cannot.

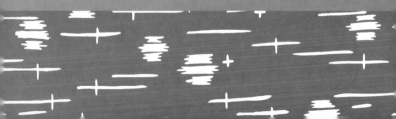

Bite off more than you can chew,
then chew it.

Ella Williams

Emotional balance tips
the scales of destiny
in your favor.

Be part of the serene creative process
going on all around you in nature.

**You cannot drift your way
to the top of a mountain.**

Use time as a tool, not as a stick with which to beat yourself.

Patience and self-control enable you to create the things you want in life while eliminating the things you don't want.

The secret of patience is managing your emotions to give yourself the time to see where they are leading you.

A young person, to achieve, must first get out of his mind any notion either of the ease or rapidity of success. Nothing ever just happens in this world.

Edward William Bok

Tolerance,
Listening,
Compassion

Compassion is the basis of patience.

With patience and commitment comes the desire to help yourself and those around you to reach their potential.

Patience has its limits.
Take it too far, and it's cowardice.

George Jackson

Never mistake patience for dispassion.

Our lives are connected by a thousand invisible threads; patience allows them to stretch rather than to break.

Patience is the ability to see others as they would wish to be seen.

Resolve never to give up on anybody.

Patience is finest when shown to those who do not deserve it.

The greatest gift we can give to another is our undivided attention.

Patience is the strongest force in the world; stronger even than love, because it expresses faith, hope, and charity.

Those without patience cannot love; those who cannot love, cannot live.

With love and
patience, nothing
is impossible.
Daisaku Ikeda

The eye sees only what the mind
is patient enough to comprehend.

If patience was more commonplace, there would be less call for it.

Patience is the understanding of and participation in diversity.

Whenever others get hurt, it is usually a sign that we have deviated from the path of patience.

Pave your path to emotional growth with good humor and compassion.

A friend who is prepared to be patient with you is one of life's greatest treasures.

You can learn many things from children. How much patience you have, for instance.

Franklin P. Jones

Compassion and patience are not signs of weakness and limitation, but manifestations of strength and resolution.

You cannot
teach a person
anything if one
of you lacks
patience.

When someone is impatient with you, it is a sign that they are only taking into consideration their needs rather than your abilities.

Never let anyone steal your patience. It is yours to give, not for others to take.

Tolerance is very infectious; so always be full of tolerance.

Apportioning blame and showing patience are mutually exclusive.

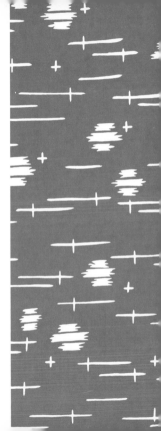

Be patient with someone, and they will do all the more.

Understand the experience of others and you will experience the understanding of others.

Don't find fault.
Find resilience.

If you have patience
and tolerance you
attract patience and
tolerance. Life does
give back in kind.

Patience makes a woman beautiful in middle age.

Elliot Paul

We must practice patience every day. Otherwise we grow intolerant.

Patience is a gift: pass it on.

The only way to learn about tolerance is to begin practicing it.

Always keep your feet on the ground in case someone needs to lean on you.

Think the best of everyone —it saves so much trouble.

Patience that does not touch and does not engage is not worth anything.

Patience and tolerance are a set—you can't have one without the other.

Remind yourself regularly that you are more capable of tolerance than you think.

Patience is the ultimate expression of love.

The most patient thing you can do for a person is to make it easier for them to accept and like themselves.

Humility is attentive patience.

Simone Weil

Impatience, like jealousy, despises the advancement of others.

The highest result of patience is tolerance.

To be sincerely patient in one direction makes us more patient in others.

The simplest way to bring out the best in people is to raise your expectations of them.

If you are genuinely interested in others, there is no room for impatience.

People are
always more
than they seem.

We can use our words and actions to lift others up or to put them down with equal effort.

A patient ear is worth a thousand tongues.

Patience is the ability to put up with people you'd like to put down.

Ulrike Ruffert

Patience does not concern itself with the "good" and "bad" of people.

If you are impatient with people, you have no time to love them.

Look for faults
and you will
always find them.

All deeds of kindness and beneficence take root in the soil of the patient heart.

The eye can only see the surface; a patient ear can see much deeper.

All ignorance is the lack of tolerance.

Never doubt those
whom you trust;
never hate those
whom you doubt.

**Aim to make friends with
everyone you meet and put
them at their ease, especially
those you find most difficult.**

The size of a person's sphere of influence corresponds with the extent of their patience and sympathy.

Patience with others is Love,
Patience with self is Hope,
Patience with God is Faith.

Adel Bestavros

Try to glimpse that from our different points of view, we are yet seeking the same truth.

Do not speak without due consideration of your audience.

When you become aware of inauthenticity in others, do not draw attention to it; observe with passive detachment and prefer forgiveness to judgment.

We cannot be happy
through life if we
cannot patiently
harmonize with all
those around us.

Patiently seek to find areas of mutual dependence and build the basis of coexistence.

When you are patient you get to hear both sides of the argument.

The patient person lets others do the talking.

Nature gave us one tongue and two ears so we could hear twice as much as we speak.

Epictatus

If you can't say anything nice, shut up and listen until you can.

Allow your priorities to be dictated by your broad-mindedness rather than your prejudices.

The more able a person, the harder they must work not to grow impatient with those who aren't as adept as they are.

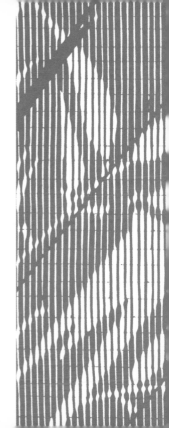

Do not cut social ties, yet do not encumber your life with hollow social obligations.

Do you want to be "right" or do you want love?

Patience cures people; both the ones who give it and the ones who receive it.

If you have been wronged, let it go. Forgive for your sake as well as theirs.

Impatience finds fault;
patience searches for a remedy.

**In the final analysis,
what will matter
most is not what
you learned but
what you taught.**

Impatience leads to loneliness; patience leads to friendship.

Like stones, words are laborious and unforgiving, and the fitting of them together, like the fitting of stones, demands great patience and strength of purpose and particular skill.

Edmund Morrison

Learn to show patience even when you don't feel it.

We are not put on this earth to see through each other, but to see each other through.

Patience is one of the most important components of love.

The best thing you can do with patience is show it.

Patience is listening without judgement.

The best way to understand people is to tolerate their imperfections while they reveal their true character to you; there is no trust without patience.

Patience is a great teacher; all learning comes through the patient sharing of knowledge and experience.

Lend someone a patient ear and you will be repaid with wisdom, trust, and respect.

There is nothing more galling to angry people than the coolness of those on whom they wish to vent their spleen.

Alexandre Dumas

A patient person closes their mouth and opens their eyes and ears.

If people won't meet you halfway, keep walking toward them; that way you will reach them even if they refuse to move; then you can invite them to walk alongside you.

The source of patience is cherishing others.

Next time you say "so, how are you?" see what happens when you are genuinely interested in the answer.

The more you are willing to listen to what others have to say, the more you realize that they may actually know what they're talking about.

Don't let the experience of others go to waste. Help is closer than you think.

The best way to learn patience is to teach it.

Come to a deeper understanding that people are human, just like you.

It's okay to believe you're right, so long as that doesn't mean that everybody else is wrong.

If you're angry at a loved one, hug that person. And mean it. You may not want to hug—which is all the more reason to do so. It's hard to stay angry when someone shows they love you, and that's precisely what happens when we hug each other.

Walter Anderson

Try to be kind and considerate to all living things; they have as much right to live as you.

Don't judge someone else until you have reached their place.

The faults we find in others are the ones we despise most in ourselves.

Don't fool yourself into believing that you are entitled to more than anyone else.

Even with the truth, there are acceptable ways to speak. Sometimes patience urges us to hold on to our truths.

Patient people never laugh at the dreams of others.

The art of love is largely the art of persistence.

Albert Ellis

The biggest compliment you can pay someone is your patience.

Instead of getting impatient at people and circumstances, try to understand them.

Just because you have an opinion doesn't mean that others should share it.

Have the humility to recognize that we are all works-in-progress.

Never discourage anyone who
continually makes progress,
no matter how slow.

**Conquer the angry man
or woman by patient
understanding.**

If you can't stand someone,
sit down and listen to them
until you can.

The hands of time are kind to those who sew their love with patience.

Heather Harpham Kopp

Make others your overriding concern.

A patient enemy is better than an impatient friend.

If you can't beat them, show them some respect: they must have figured something out that you haven't.

It is easier to hold court than to hold your tongue.

Do not make the mistake of thinking that everyone is just like you, or that they are so very different.

Patience is listening to someone talk about themselves when you want to talk about yourself.

Self-reverence, self-knowledge,
self-control—these three alone
lead life to sovereign power.

Lord Alfred Tennyson

**You can't put yourself in
someone else's shoes until
you take off your own.**

Misunderstandings are the logical
consequences of impatient words.

**Patience is remaining open to all
points of view instead of rigidly
fixating on only one.**

How you treat yourself is how you invite others to treat you.

Seek first to understand, and then to be understood.

Stephen Covey

When you look beyond the imperfections, everyone is perfect.

Never
Surrender

Most of the important things in the world are achieved by those who have the confidence, the resolve, and the patience to continue long after everyone else has quit and gone home.

Patience gives us strength to endure.

Life can be an adventure in forbearance.

The strongest of all warriors are these two—Time and Patience.

Leo Tolstoy

Patience is an underground spring that never runs dry.

The mystery of existence is the connection between what we are willing to endure and for how long.

Stop complaining and use that time for thinking or doing.

The difference
between
perseverance
and obstinacy is
that one often
comes from a
strong will, and
the other from a
strong won't.

Henry Ward
Beecher

Nature is serene: the sun shines equally over the good and the evil; the moon reflects its light while they sleep. The rain falls on everyone and the seasons are impartial. Take strength from nature and recognize that there is dynamism in fortitude.

Develop the
patience to live
beneath your means.

If you want to get out, you always have to go through.

Patient people take over where others stop, and then go on to claim the prize.

You're only a failure if you give up too early; if you give something your all and you still fail to achieve your goal, at least you can't spend the rest of your life asking "What if?"

How many a man has thrown
up his hands at a time when
a little more effort, a little more
patience would have achieved
success?

Elbert Green Hubbard

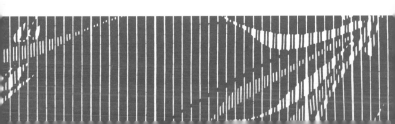

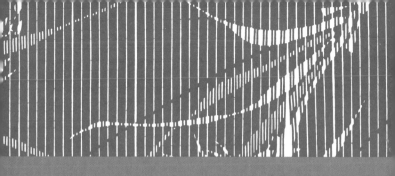

So long as your patience
and compassion are
invincible, your spirit will
never be beaten.

You never know the limits of your patience until someone tests them.

Ninety-nine percent of the failures come from people who lack just one percent more patience.

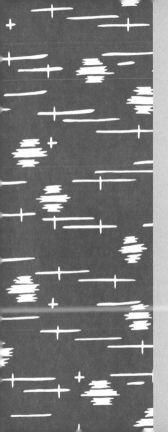

When on the brink of complete discouragement, success is discerning that the line between failure and success is so fine that often a single extra effort is all that is needed to bring victory out of defeat.

Elbert Green Hubbard

Without patience there is little incentive to give everything your best effort in the face of stiff opposition.

Patience requires us to toil without making excuses or complaints.

Necessity may be the mother of invention, but doggedness is certainly the father.

None appear as worn-out and broken as those who have lost their staying power.

Patience is bitter, but its fruit is sweet.

Aristotle

Whatever you do, don't do half of it.

**Make
patience
your religion.**

Don't give up
so long as
you still have
a goal; and if
you don't
have a goal,
get one.

Patience means
self-suffering.
Gandhi

Accept tough challenges with enthusiasm and then overcome them with quiet self-possession.

Don't be daunted by the wait; it's later than you think.

Great works are performed, not by strength, but by perseverance.

Samuel Johnson

Work at being patient; it is the most useful exercise.

Nobody ever died of too much patience.

Patience means never giving up on anybody.

A patient spirit is stronger than anything that can happen to it.

Health and patience mutually beget each other.

Be patient. It is a way of being wise.

Nothing can defend itself against unwavering patience.

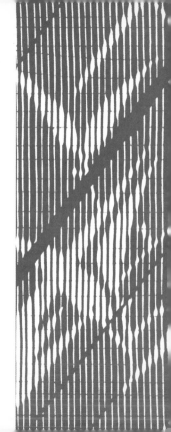

It is easier to find men who will volunteer to die, than to find those who are willing to endure pain with patience.

Julius Caesar

Change is unavoidable and inevitable. Patience helps us to accept the truth of transience.

Impatience is to walk barefoot along life's road, feeling the pain of every stone.

A person's worth is no greater than their fortitude.

With enough patience nothing is too much trouble.

Don't be sad, don't be angry, if life deceives you! Submit to your grief—your time for joy will come, believe me.

Alexander Pushkin

Do not accept that impatience is an unavoidable component of modern life.

The surest sign of impatience is loneliness.

Learn to work hard and wait softly.

How long are you prepared to work to make your dreams come true? As long as it takes?

If patience is worth anything, it must endure to the end of time. And a living faith will last in the midst of the blackest storm.

Gandhi

The rhythm of life can't always be a *bossa nova*.

Perseverance is fundamentally different from stubbornness; patience is yielding and arises through knowledge; stubbornness is hard and is the consequence of the lack of knowledge.

The greatest achievements of your life lie ahead of you, but they can only be reached with persistence.

Impatience criticizes the growing conditions; patience sows the seeds of change.

Things turn out best for those who do not complain with the way things are turning out.

If praying is the highest expression of human thought, then complaining is the lowest.

All suffering is the result of the mind clinging to its impatient thoughts.

Accept things you cannot change with humor and grace.

The longer the grind, the finer the flour.

Success is generally due to holding on, and failure to letting go.

A mule will labor ten years willingly and patiently for you, for the privilege of kicking you once.

William Faulkner

Patience is the path of unrelenting diligence.

Removing impatience frees
you from pain and suffering.

**Tolerance is never
a sign of weakness.**

Those who give up too early in their search for answers invariably resort to superstition.

With persistence, anything can become second nature.

The few who persevere become the envy of the many who quit early.

Nothing is as easy as it first appears.

Things
turn out
best
when you
make the
best of
the way
things
turn out.

My son, observe the postage stamp! Its usefulness depends upon its ability to stick to one thing until it gets there.

Henry Wheeler Shaw

Patience is the cornerstone of self-discipline.

Patience is not the complete absence of impatience, but the ability to cope with it.

Patience and faith are two sides of the same coin.

Without patience, walking one mile feels the same as walking twenty.

Those with patience know that they will not have to wait forever; those without feel like they already have.

Common sense tells us that hitting one's head against a wall is painful and pointless; it's the same with impatience.

She who loves roses must be patient and not cry out when she is pierced by thorns.

Olga Brouman

Patience is wanting
no longer to punish
those who hurt us.

**Don't use suffering as
an excuse to stop trying.**

Only give up if you are willing to settle
for a dead end instead of a destination.

**If you want a better life you must be
prepared to give up certain things:
starting with your excuses.**

Pay more attention
to the good stuff.

There will always be a million reasons why you failed, but only one if you succeed—patience.

With patience and forgiveness all past wounds can be healed.

Never start a sentence with "Yes, but…"

Don't complain— your life isn't over yet.

All suffering comes from craving.

Difficulties are meant to rouse, not discourage. The human spirit is to grow strong by conflict.

William Ellery Channing

The lowest moments in our lives can lead to our greatest triumphs.

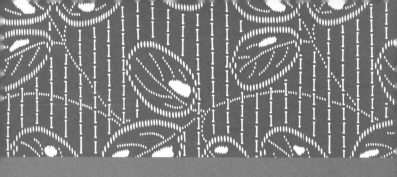

**Regardless of how many times
you fall, keep on getting up.**

Anything can be fixed
with the correct tools.

**Whenever you fall down,
try to pick something up.**

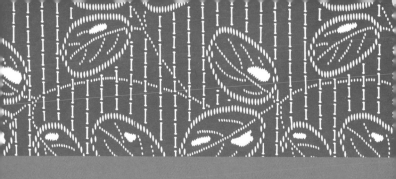

Put off pleasure until your work is finished but avoid mindless pleasures. Find enjoyment in your work but don't toil so hard that you have no occasion for delight.

The most assertive act one can perform is to be patient.

Running away from where you do not want to be, and walking in the direction of where you do, are not the same thing.

Whoever said anybody has a right to give up?

Marian Wright Edelman

Sometimes doing your best involves enduring hardship, misfortune, provocation, and pain.

Patience is like a raft, with which you should plot a course through the flood of your frustration.

Impatience is a confession of pain.

Do not overreact to circumstances which are outside of your control, nor to those which aren't.

Impatience casts a long shadow.

Unless you have linked
yourself to true acceptance
you will never understand.

The Art of Patience

**Most people achieved their
greatest success one step
beyond what looked like their
greatest failure.**

Brian Tracy

Never stop forging
the steel of patience.

**Sometimes patience
requires nonresistance;
at other times it requires
resistance; the skill lies in
spotting the difference.**

Patience is a lifestyle, not a technique.

Patience is a struggle for balance between the mystical and the mundane.

You need patience to spot a shooting star, and sometimes even a break in the clouds.

When the world around you is in disorder, when your thoughts and desires come to nothing, when loved ones pass from you, and barrenness seems to enclose you—just believe.

Patience is the light that perseveres through the night.

Focus and feel your emotions completely so you can release them.

When patience and truth come together, they withstand all challenges.

The difference between successful people and unsuccessful people is that successful people fail many more times than unsuccessful people.

There is nothing you can ever achieve or gain that you cannot lose, in a matter of seconds.

If you try, you'll either succeed or fail. If you don't try, you'll fail anyway.

It costs a lot to be patient but the dividends are priceless.

People are as impatient as they choose to be.

Sometimes you have to go where you don't want to go, to get where you need to be.

There are more people in the world who are afraid of life than those who are afraid of death.

When in doubt,
do without.

Expectations are
premeditated resentments.

When life turns upside down, there's always a better solution than standing on your head.

Behind the clouds the sun is still shining.

The thing that poker and life have in common is that you don't have to be dealt the best hand to win.

Life's tough, so stop complaining and get a helmet.

Learn from pain.

Procrastination kills time; patience resurrects it.

Complaint is not a force for change, and therefore it is a waste of time.

Remember, you only have to succeed the last time.

Brian Tracy

An Hachette Livre UK Company

First published in Great Britain by MQ Publications
a division of Octopus Publishing Group Ltd
2–4 Heron Quays, London, E14 4JP
www.octopusbooks.co.uk

Distributed in the United States and Canada by
Hachette Book Group USA
237 Park Avenue
New York
NY 10017

ISBN 13 978-1-84601-285-3
ISBN 10 1-84601-285-6

A CIP catalogue record for this book is available from
the British Library.

10 9 8 7 6 5 4 3 2 1

Printed and bound in China